THE KLUTZ BOOK OF PAPER AIRPLANES

by Doug Stillinger

KLUTZ

KLUTZ creates activity books and other great stuff for kids ages 3 to 103. We began our corporate life in 1977 in a garage we shared with a Chevrolet Impala. Although we've outgrown that first office, Klutz galactic headquarters remains in Palo Alto, California, and we're still staffed entirely by real human beings. For those of you who collect mission statements, here's ours:

Create Wonderful things • Be good • Have fun

WRITE US
We would love to hear your comments regarding this or any of our books. We have many!

KLUTZ.
450 Lambert Avenue
Palo Alto, CA 94306

Printed in the USA. 75
©2004 Klutz. All rights reserved.

Published by Klutz, a subsidiary of Scholastic Inc. Scholastic and associated logos are trademarks and/or registered trademarks of Scholastic Inc. Klutz and associated logos are trademarks and/or registered trademarks of Klutz. No part of this publication may be reproduced in any form or by any means without written permission of Klutz.

Distributed in the UK by
Scholastic UK Ltd, Westfield Road
Southam, Warwickshire, England CV47 0RA

Distributed in Australia by
Scholastic Australia Customer Service
PO Box 579, Gosford, NSW Australia 2250

ISBN 978-1-59174-900-4
4158570888

VISIT OUR WEBSITE
You can check out all the stuff we make, find a nearby retailer, request a catalog, sign up for a newsletter, e-mail us or just goof off!

www.klutz.com

the planes

10 NAKAMURA LOCK

14 SPY PLANE

18 SWASHBUCKLER

26 HEADHUNTER

30 THE HAMMER

36 PTEROPLANE

40 THE PROFESSIONAL

46 FLYING NINJA

50 SPACE CRUISER

54 THE HURRICANE

forget everything you know about paper airplanes!

These aren't paper toys. And they're only technically paper airplanes. These are high-performance, blow-the-competition-away flying paper *machines*.

The ten planes in this book are for people who think they've seen a good paper plane or two. They're for the hard to impress, the playground veterans — the kid at the next desk who thinks he and his plane will get sent to the principal's office first. These are the planes that can prove him wrong.

MATERIALS

All you need to make every plane in this book is a pair of hands, a smooth surface and a piece of paper.

Use 8 ½ x 11-inch (21.6 x 27.9 -cm) paper with no cuts, tears, or holes in it. Photocopy and printer paper make a fine plane. Regular binder paper, with lines and three holes, is not flightworthy. We don't recommend it.

read this page!

If you skip this page, your planes won't work. It's that simple.

1 MAKE GREAT FOLDS

Great planes start with great folding. Take your time and put the paper exactly where it needs to be. Perfect folding will save a bad throw, but no throw in the world will save sloppy folding.

EXACT FOLDS WILL FLY

SLOPPY FOLDS WON'T FLY

2 CHECK SYMMETRY

Every plane in this book is the same on both sides. The left wing is always a mirror image of the right wing. If you fold your plane so that one side is even the tiniest bit different from the other side, your plane won't fly straight, if it flies at all. The golden rule is this: *If you make a mistake, make the exact same mistake on the other side.*

The difference is symmetry. Look carefully.

THIS PLANE FLIES GREAT

THIS PLANE CRASHES GREAT

3 THROW IT EASY

Make your first few throws light and breezy. No matter how good your folding is, we guarantee that your plane's maiden flight will also be its maiden crash. Once you get it flying okay, then you can open up and haul off.

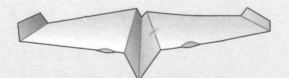

4 TOSS, CHECK & TWEAK

If you make your plane and it doesn't fly great right off (and it won't), you'll need to tweak the wings. **After every throw,** → check:

1. Symmetry

2. The Dihedral (Wing Angle) (see page 9)

3. Elevators and Ailerons (see page 9)

A WELL-FOLDED AIRPLANE THAT HAS BEEN TESTED AND TWEAKED WILL FLY LIKE THIS...

A WELL-FOLDED PLANE THAT HASN'T BEEN TESTED AND TWEAKED WILL PROBABLY FLY LIKE THIS...

DOWN...DOWN....

5 IF ALL ELSE FAILS, FOLD ANOTHER

Some planes look perfect but, no matter how much you fuss, they just won't fly. Our advice? Grab another sheet and make a new one.

Stare at your plane, right down the middle. Make sure it looks the same on both sides and that the wings are angled upward.

folding

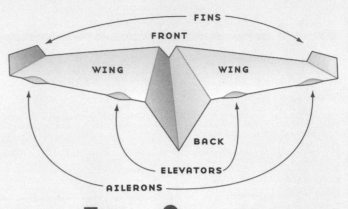

and tweaking

Great folding makes a plane fly great. Sloppy folding makes a big, flightless mess. Take your time and fold carefully and exactly.

1 ### EDGE-TO-EDGE, CORNER-TO-CORNER

Almost every fold in this book is an edge-to-edge, corner-to-corner or edge-to-crease fold. When you're making these folds, put each edge or corner precisely where it's supposed to go. Even near-misses, if there are enough of them, will ruin a plane.

2 ### CREASE WELL

With every fold, make the crease as sharp and clean as you can get it. Run your fingernail along the crease to get it flat. The better the crease, the easier the following folds will be and the better the plane will fly.

3 ### SMOOSH DOWN PAPER BUBBLES

A few folds into a plane, you may see some part of the paper bulging up. We recommend flattening these to make the rest of the folds easier. The best way is to use a pencil or pen cap and, pressing hard, sweep across the bubbled-up paper.

If your plane is folded correctly, but doesn't fly very well, you'll need to fuss with it a bit. Here's how.

DIHEDRAL

"Dihedral" is engineer-speak for the angle between a plane's wings. Every winged plane in this book flies best with a positive dihedral. That means that if you look at your plane from the back, the wings and body form a  shape. What this means to paper airplanes is this:

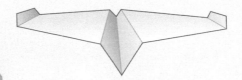

THIS PLANE FLIES   **THIS PLANE CRASHES**

ELEVATORS

Elevators are small flaps in a plane's wings that make the plane go up and down. If you want your plane to fly higher or longer, add up elevators. If it's flying too high and then diving, like it's on a rollercoaster, then it needs down elevators.

TO MAKE AN ELEVATOR, PINCH THE BACK EDGE OF A WING, NEAR THE MIDDLE FOLD. THEN BEND THE PINCHED PAPER UP OR DOWN. MAKE ANOTHER ONE ON THE OPPOSITE WING.

UP ELEVATOR
PINCH AND BEND UP. END UP LIKE THIS.

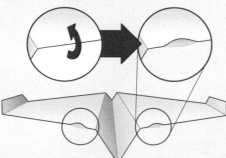

DOWN ELEVATOR
PINCH AND BEND DOWN. END UP LIKE THIS.

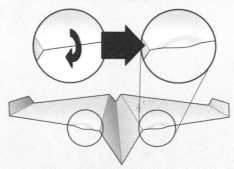

THESE FLAPS MAKE THE PLANE RISE   **THESE FLAPS MAKE THE PLANE FALL**

AILERONS

Ailerons look just like elevators, but make the plane bank or roll. An aileron in the right wing of a plane will make it bank (and turn) left, while an aileron in the left wing makes it bank (and turn) right. You make them just like you make elevators, but at the ends of the wings, not the middle.

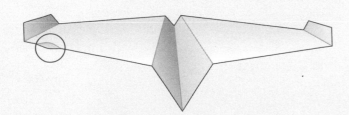

THIS PLANE TURNS RIGHT

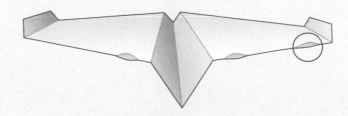

THIS PLANE TURNS LEFT

TYPE: **glider/dart**

FOLDING DIFFICULTY: **1**

FLY ZONE:

indoor 🏠

outdoor ☀

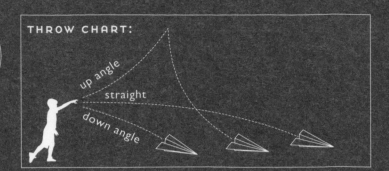

THROW CHART:

up angle

straight

down angle

The Nakamura Lock

The Nakamura Lock is **easy to fold** and plenty forgiving. But the best part? Chances are, this will be the **best-flying** paper airplane you've ever made.

1

start
like
this

2

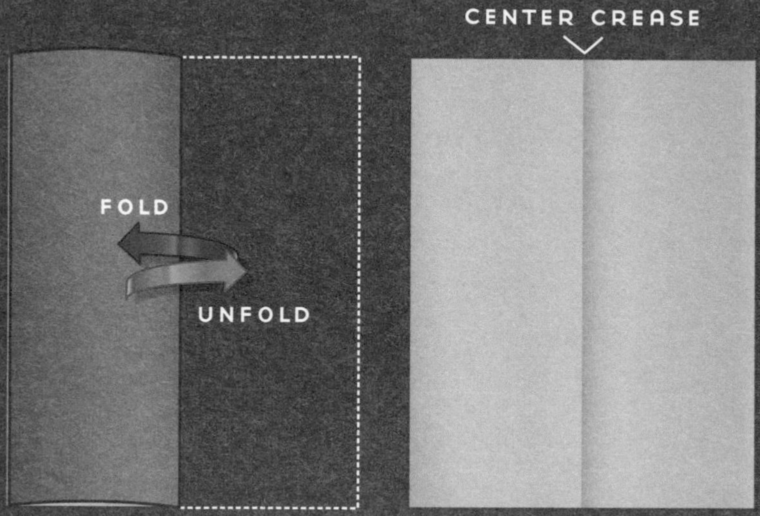

FOLD

UNFOLD

Fold in half lengthwise.
Unfold to make a
center crease.

CENTER CREASE

end up
like
this

3

FOLD

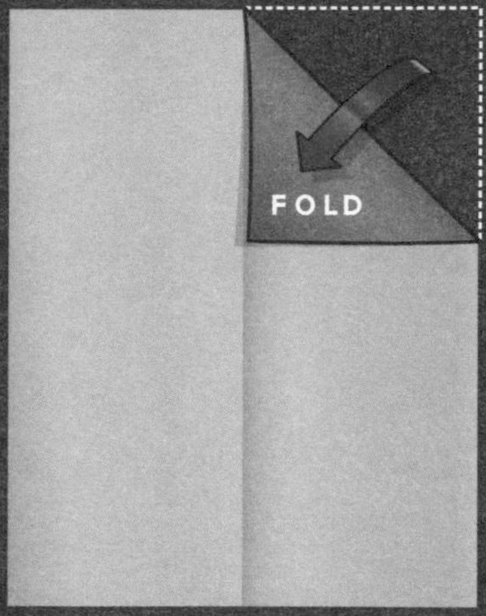

Fold the upper-right
corner down so the
top edge sits on the
center crease.

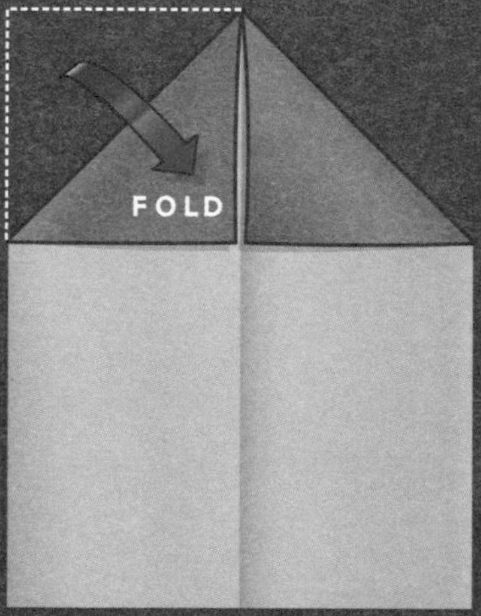

FOLD

Do the same with the
upper-left corner.

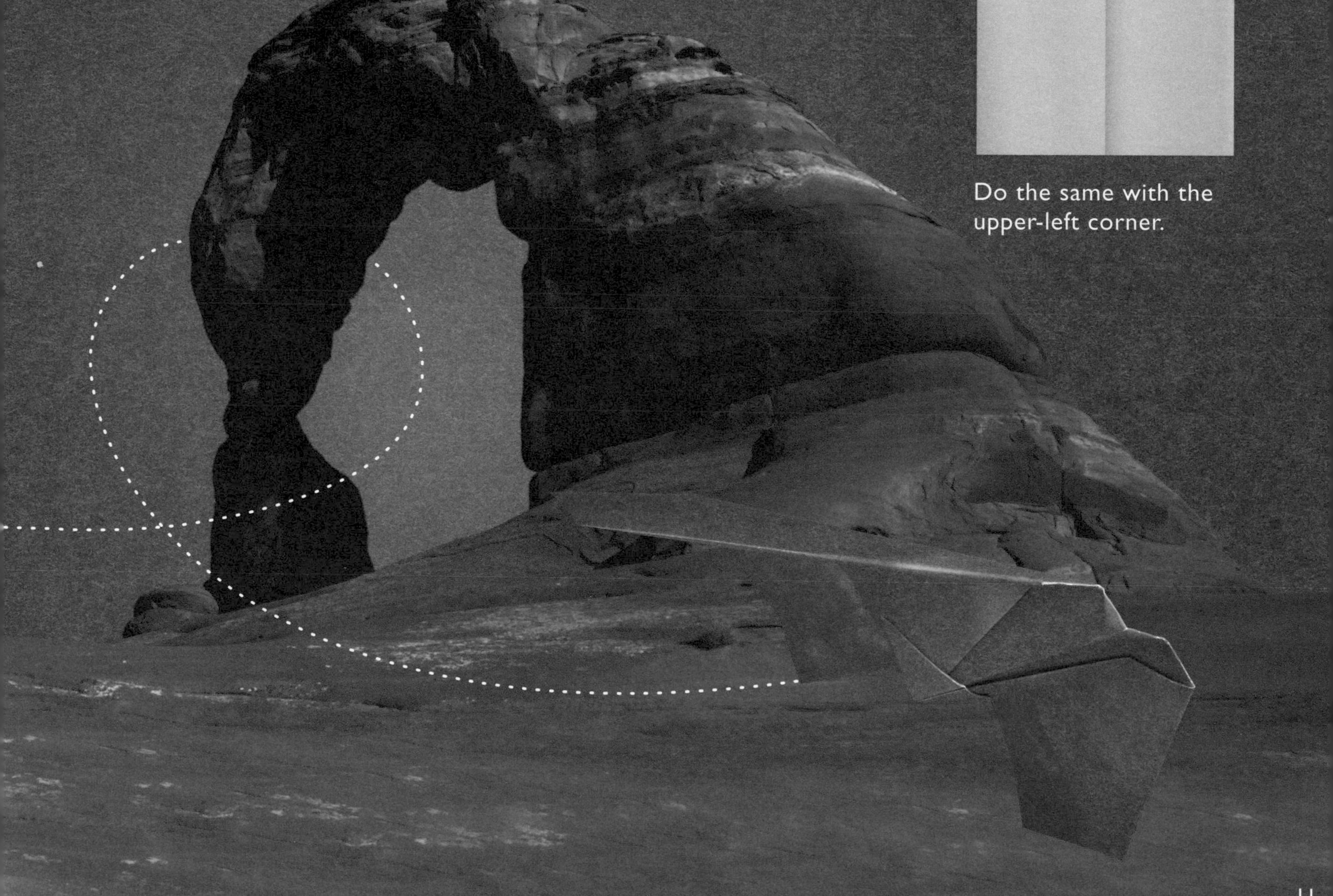

4

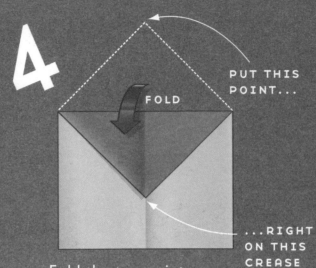

PUT THIS POINT...

FOLD

...RIGHT ON THIS CREASE

Fold the top point down, creasing right beneath the flaps you just made.

5

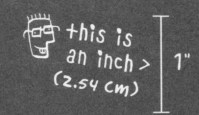

this is an inch > 1"
(2.54 cm)

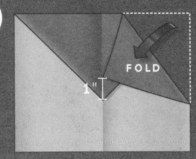

FOLD

1"

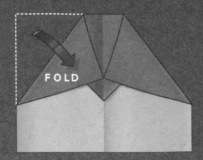

FOLD

Put the upper-right corner on the center crease, about 1 inch (2.54 cm) above the point. Crease well.

Do the same with the upper-left corner.

folding tip   Be precise!

6

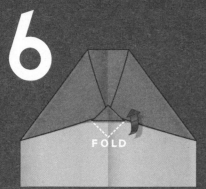

flip over

end up like this

Flip the point up and fold so it's right on the center crease.

7

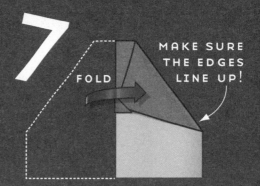

FOLD

MAKE SURE THE EDGES LINE UP!

Fold in half. Make sure the edges of the left side line up perfectly with the edges on the right.

8

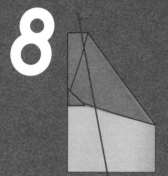

end up like this

Fold just the top flap so that the crease falls on the red line shown.

flip over

9

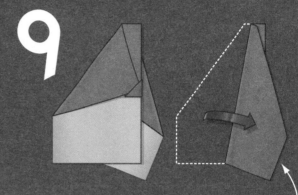

Fold the other wing so that it sits right on top of the first one.

LINE UP THE EDGES WITH THE WING YOU JUST MADE

ALMOST FINISHED

Unfold the wings part way, so that your plane looks like this from the back.

 FLYING THE NAKAMURA LOCK
This classic paper plane flies best with a light, straight-ahead toss.

TYPE: glider

FOLDING DIFFICULTY: **1**

FLY ZONE:
indoor 🏠
outdoor ☀

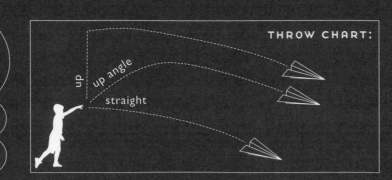

THROW CHART:

up
up angle
straight

Spy Plane

The Spy Plane
flies higher and
longer than most
planes in this book.
If you've got a big,
open space and a healthy
throwing arm, this is
your plane.

1

start
like
this

2

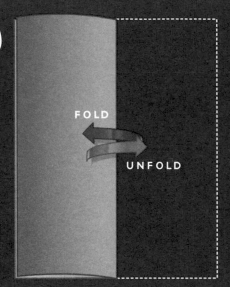

FOLD

UNFOLD

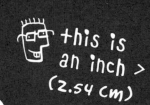
end up
like
this

Fold it in half lengthwise. Unfold to make a center crease.

**TIP
good folding =
good flying!**

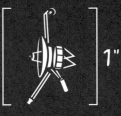
**this is
an inch >**
(2.54 cm)

1"

3

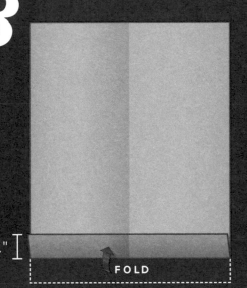

1"

FOLD

Then, fold the bottom inch of the page up, putting the center crease right on top of itself.

4

**PUT THIS CREASE
EXACTLY ON THE
ONE UNDERNEATH
IT. DO THIS FOR
EACH FOLD.**

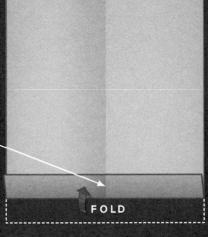

FOLD

Make the same fold six more times...

7 folds total

Roughly 2" (5.08 cm)

end up
like
this

...until you get this.

15

5 rotate

flip over

6  Fold in half, from left to right.

1"

7 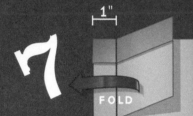 Fold the top flap back along the red line as shown. FOLD

folding tip match the edges and press hard!

8 flip over

Fold the left side over to make the other wing. Line it up with the wing underneath.

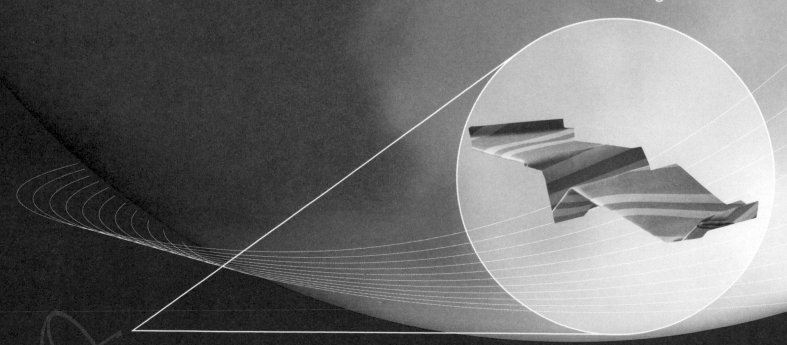

ALMOST FINISHED

Partially unfold so that your plane looks like this from the back.

Then put thumb-width fins in each wing. Fold them parallel to the body.

 FLYING THE SPY PLANE
Throw the Spy Plane straight up and as hard as you can. When it peaks out, its nose will flop over and the plane will glide to the ground. The higher you get the Spy Plane before it starts gliding, the longer it will stay in the air.

Swashbuckler

TYPE: stunt

FOLDING DIFFICULTY: 2

FLY ZONE:
- ✔ indoor 🏠
- ✔ outdoor ☀

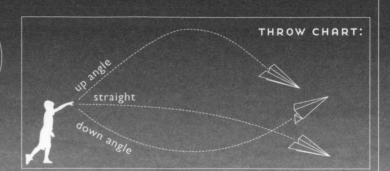

THROW CHART:

up angle
straight
down angle

THE Swashbuckler

The ultimate stunt plane! It's hard to throw badly, harder to fold wrong, and almost impossible to get a bad flight out of it. If you only remember how to make one plane in this book, make this it!

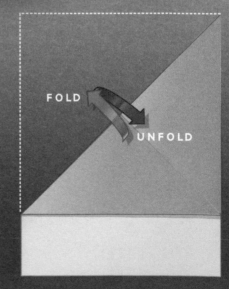

1

start like this

Pick up this corner and put it near the **X**.

X

2

LINE THESE EDGES UP!

FOLD
UNFOLD

Make a perfect diagonal crease. Then unfold it.

FOLD
UNFOLD

Do the same thing with the other corner. Fold and unfold.

3

flip over

end up like this

You should now have a big creased X in your paper.

4

Fold the top of your paper down so that the corners line up precisely with the bottom of the creased X. Unfold.

5

flip over

PRESS HERE... AND THE SIDES WILL POP UP

After you flip the paper over, lay it down on the table.

Then, press the middle of the creased X until the sides "jump" up.

6

BRING THE SIDES FORWARD AND TOGETHER

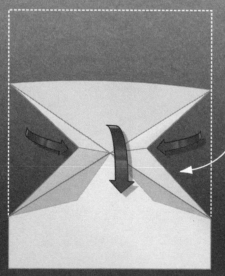

end up like this

good folding = good flying!

Pull the top edge of the paper downward. As you do, the sides of the paper should fold inward along the horizontal creases you already made.

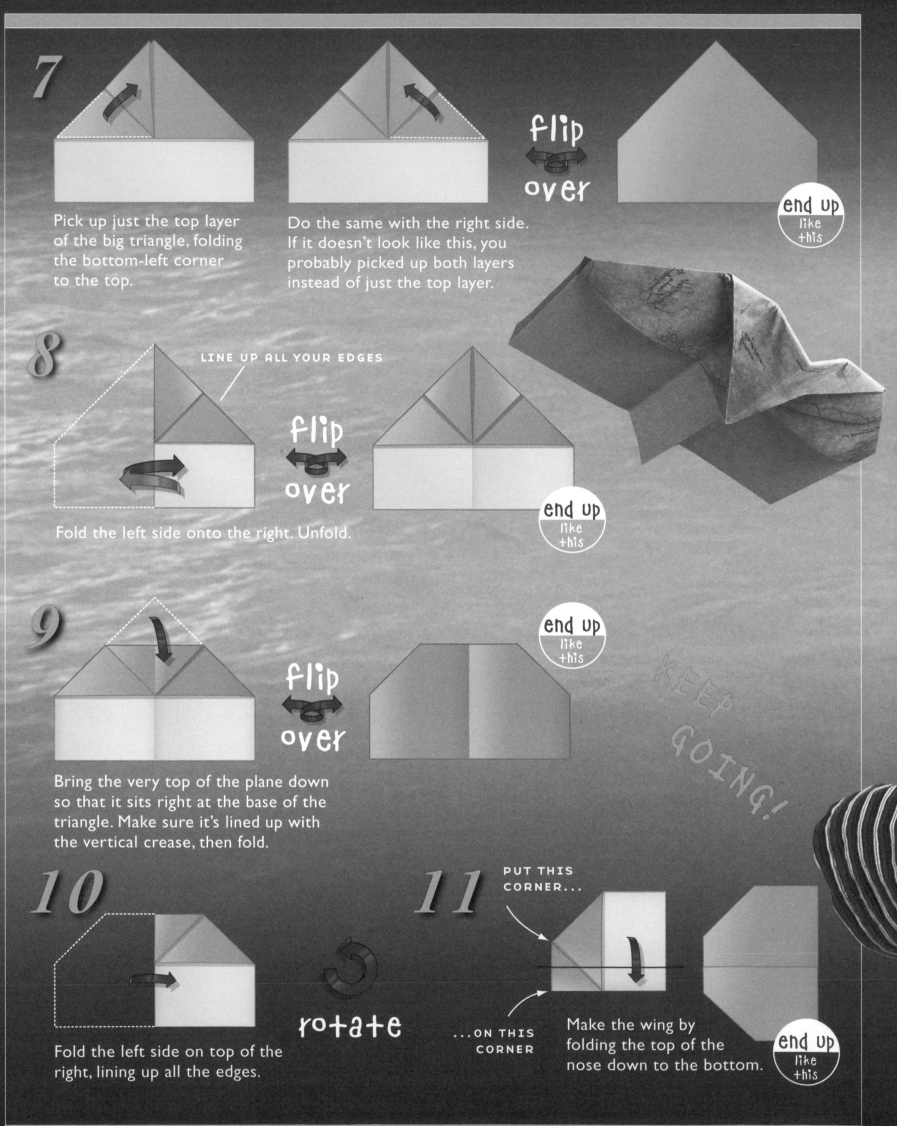

7

Pick up just the top layer of the big triangle, folding the bottom-left corner to the top.

Do the same with the right side. If it doesn't look like this, you probably picked up both layers instead of just the top layer.

flip over

end up like this

8

LINE UP ALL YOUR EDGES

flip over

Fold the left side onto the right. Unfold.

end up like this

9

flip over

end up like this

Bring the very top of the plane down so that it sits right at the base of the triangle. Make sure it's lined up with the vertical crease, then fold.

KEEP GOING!

10

rotate

Fold the left side on top of the right, lining up all the edges.

11

PUT THIS CORNER...

...ON THIS CORNER

Make the wing by folding the top of the nose down to the bottom.

end up like this

12

flip over

end up like this

13

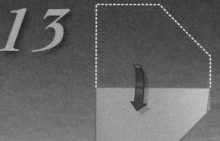

PUT ONE EDGE RIGHT ON TOP OF THE OTHER

Flip your plane over and do the same thing to the other wing. Line up the bottom edges of the wings.

Unfold so that your plane looks like this from the back.

ALMOST FINISHED

Finally, add pinky-width fins to the ends of your wings. Make them straight up and down.

 FLYING THE SWASHBUCKLER

Big, swooping loops and turns are no trouble at all for the Swashbuckler. Throw the plane upward at a diagonal and put a little weight behind it. If your folds are clean, you may get great flights right off. If not, put tiny elevators in the wings to help with the swooping and looping.

learning to fly

Getting your plane into the air isn't hard, but getting great flights one after another can take a little practice. The trick is to figure out what type of plane you're throwing and how you want it to fly. Then, give it the launch it needs to get there.

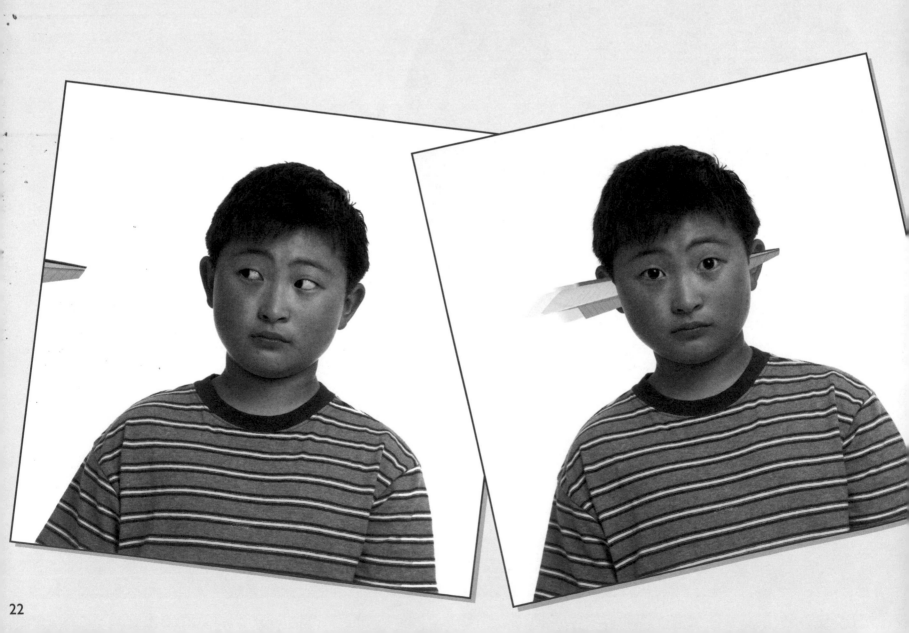

The only **2 things** that make one throw different from another are **speed and angle**. And the way a plane is designed, it will naturally "like" certain angles and speeds, but not others. Dart-shaped planes, since they're thin and sleek, like fast throws. Gliders, with their wide, flat shape, prefer slow ones. In fact, for most planes, **all you need to know are these (big, important) rules:**

big, important throwing Speed Rules:

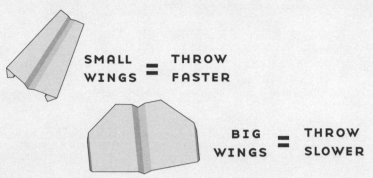

SMALL WINGS **=** THROW FASTER

BIG WINGS **=** THROW SLOWER

big, important throwing Angle Rules:

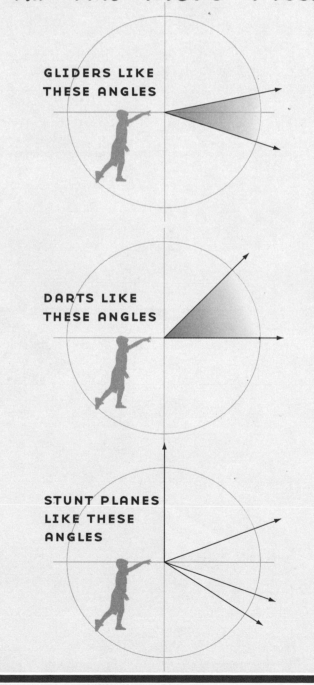

GLIDERS LIKE THESE ANGLES

DARTS LIKE THESE ANGLES

STUNT PLANES LIKE THESE ANGLES

FLYING GLIDERS

Gliders glide. They're built for long, slow flights and big, lazy turns. A good glider, with a good launch, almost never lands without hitting something first.

There are two kinds of gliders: high fliers and room-crossers. Most gliders are of the room-crossing variety and are best flown with a smooth, even launch. You're pushing, not throwing, the plane so there's no wind-up and no such thing as launching it too slow. In fact, the rule of thumb is this: Launch a glider at the same angle and speed it would go if it were already flying.

High fliers begin with a rocket launch before gliding back to earth. Throw them straight up, like you're going to put a baseball on the moon.

THE PROFESSIONAL

THE SPACE CRUISER

THE SPY PLANE

THE NAKAMURA LOCK

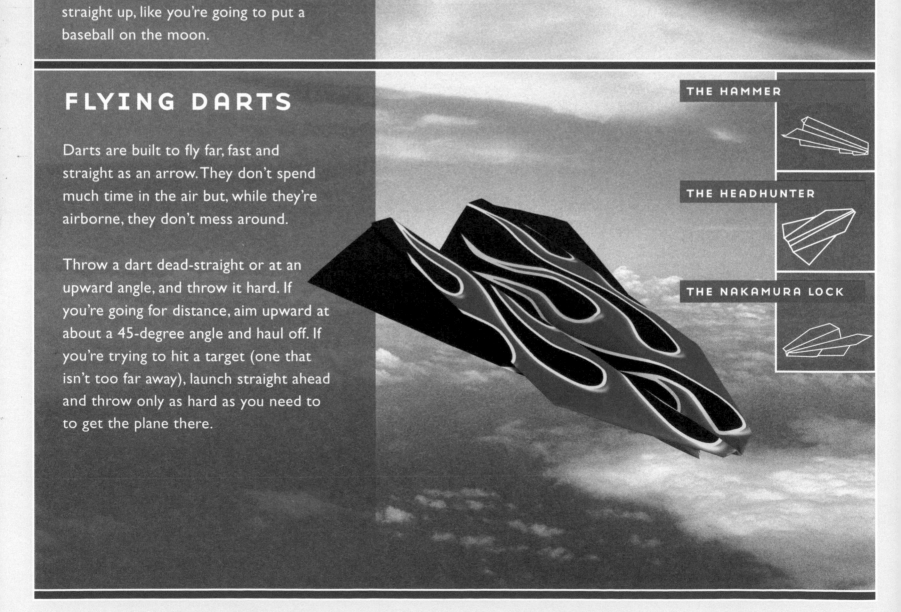

FLYING DARTS

Darts are built to fly far, fast and straight as an arrow. They don't spend much time in the air but, while they're airborne, they don't mess around.

Throw a dart dead-straight or at an upward angle, and throw it hard. If you're going for distance, aim upward at about a 45-degree angle and haul off. If you're trying to hit a target (one that isn't too far away), launch straight ahead and throw only as hard as you need to to get the plane there.

THE HAMMER

THE HEADHUNTER

THE NAKAMURA LOCK

FLYING STUNT PLANES

Stunt planes are the dogfighters of the paper airplane world. They loop, circle, dive and roll better than any other plane. They also spend a lot of time on roofs and in trees.

Stunt planes are designed to be thrown in all kinds of ways. Most do well with a medium-sized throw, up and away from you. Throw hard enough to get them to do a trick or two before they land, but not so hard that the wings bend or collapse.

How to get Loops

To get your stunt plane to loop, first give it big up elevators (see page 9). Then give it a good throw either at an angle toward the ground or directly upward.

UPWARD-THROW LOOP

DOWNWARD-THROW LOOP

How to get Circles

Circles are sideways loops. To get your plane to circle, launch it so that its wings are banked to the right, like so:

Putting an aileron in one wing can help your plane circle (see page 9).

THE FLYING NINJA

THE PROFESSIONAL

THE PTEROPLANE

THE SWASHBUCKLER

INDOOR VERSUS OUTDOOR FLIGHT

INDOOR
If you're flying indoors, you're best off with planes that need calm air but don't need much space. Darts and slow gliders work best.

OUTDOOR
Outside, you'll get the best flights from heavier, more rugged planes. Stunt planes, small darts and high-flying gliders should make up your fleet.

TYPE: **dart**

FOLDING DIFFICULTY: **3**

FLY ZONE: ✓ indoor 🏠

outdoor ☀

up angle

straight

Yikes!

+he HEAD-HUNTER

The Headhunter is sleek, fast and deadly accurate. Guaranteed to hit the chalkboard from the back of the classroom, or smack the center of the theatre screen. If any plane in this book is going to land you in trouble, this is probably it.

1

start like this

2

FOLD

UNFOLD

CENTER CREASE ↓

end up like this

Fold in half lengthwise. Unfold.

3

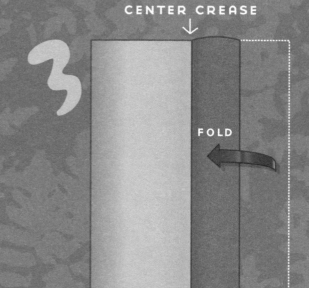

CENTER CREASE

FOLD

Fold the right edge to the center crease...

4

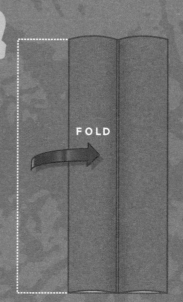

FOLD

...and do the same with the left.

5

FOLD   FOLD

Fold the top two corners down so the top edge sits right on the center crease.

6

HOLD HERE...

FOLD UP

...AND PULL THIS FLAP AS FAR AS IT WILL GO

flip over

end up like this

Hold down the flaps you just made with your finger. Then pull the big flap on the right side up from the inside corner.

7

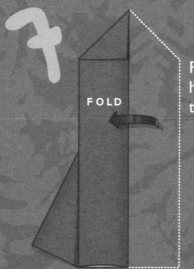

FOLD

Fold the right half over onto the left side.

8

open up

FOLD UP

Fold just the top big flap over, so it's right on top of the other one. Match up all edges perfectly.

Open up the whole thing and lay it flat.

27

9 Then, starting about 1 inch below the small triangle flaps...

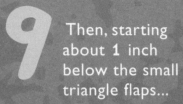

+his is an inch > | 1"
(2.54 cm)

FOLD   1"

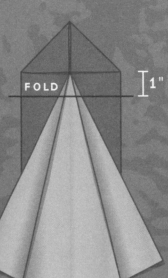

FOLD

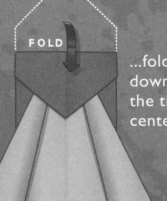

...fold the top down, putting the tip on the center crease.

POINT TOUCHES TOP

10

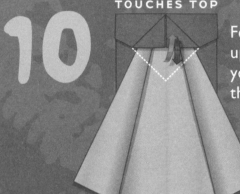

Fold the point up to the crease you just made, then unfold.

NEW CREASE MEETS CENTER CREASE

11

FOLD   FOLD

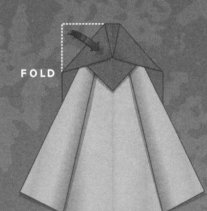

Put the top-right corner on the new crease, right in the middle.

Do the same with the left corner.

flying tip! to get longer flights, put elevators on the Headhunter's wings (see page 9).

12

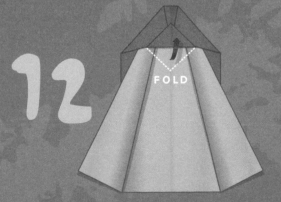

FOLD

Flip the point up, putting it on the center crease.

13 flip over

end up like this

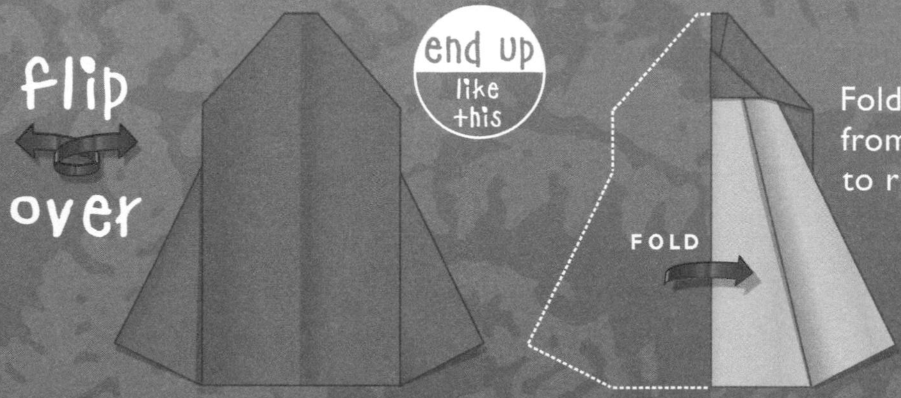

Fold in half, from left to right.

FOLD

14 FOLD

end up like this

Fold the wing along the red line.

LINE UP THIS EDGE... ...WITH THIS EDGE

15 flip over

After flipping it over...

...fold the second wing by lining the edges up with the wing below it.

ALMOST FINISHED

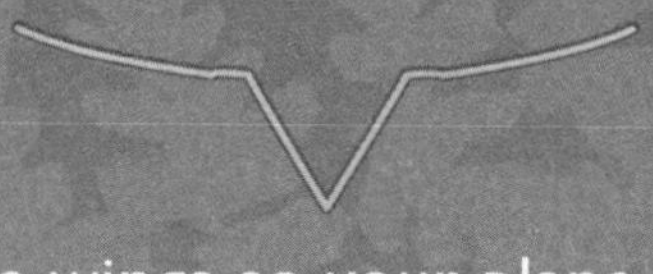

Unfold the wings so your plane looks like this from the back. Now test, fly and trim!

FLYING THE HEADHUNTER
With a little trimming, the Headhunter will be the straightest-flying plane you've ever thrown. Make sure your Headhunter looks the same on both sides, and throw straight ahead.

TYPE: **dart**

FOLDING DIFFICULTY: **5**

FLY ZONE: ✓ indoor 🏠
✓ outdoor ☀

The Hammer

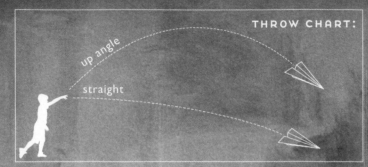

THROW CHART:

up angle

straight

THE HAMMER

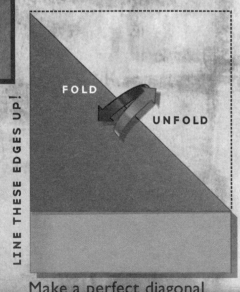

THE HAMMER IS EQUAL PARTS PAPER AIRPLANE AND ROCKET JET.

SMALL, TOUGH AND UNFAIRLY FAST, THIS IS THE RIDE OF CHOICE FOR PAPER FIGHTER PILOTS. THERE SIMPLY ISN'T A BETTER WAY TO HIT TOP SPEED WITH A SHEET OF PAPER.

1

Pick up this corner and put it near the **X**.

start like this

X

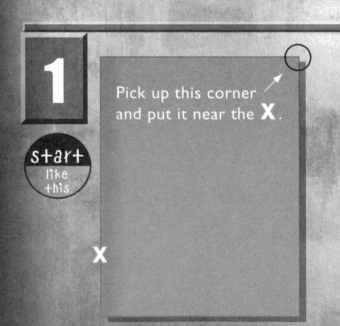

2

LINE THESE EDGES UP!

FOLD / UNFOLD

FOLD / UNFOLD

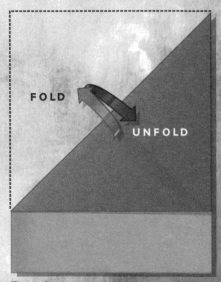

Make a perfect diagonal crease. Then unfold it.

Do the same thing with the other corner. Fold and unfold.

3

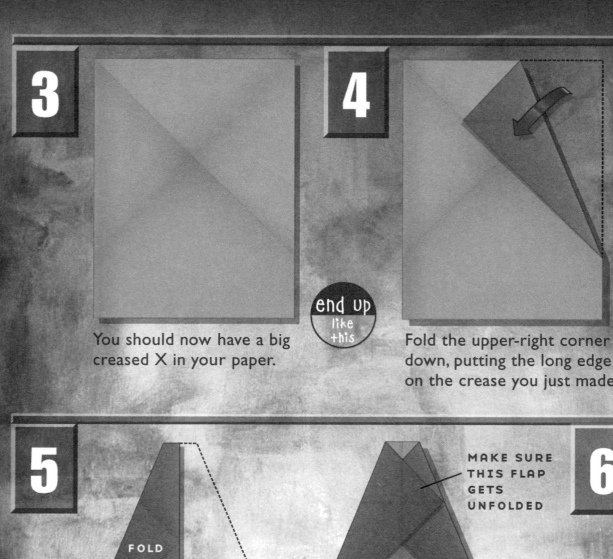

You should now have a big creased X in your paper.

end up like this

4

Fold the upper-right corner down, putting the long edge on the crease you just made.

Make the same fold with the upper-left corner.

5

FOLD

UNFOLD

Fold in half, then unfold.

MAKE SURE THIS FLAP GETS UNFOLDED

end up like this

6

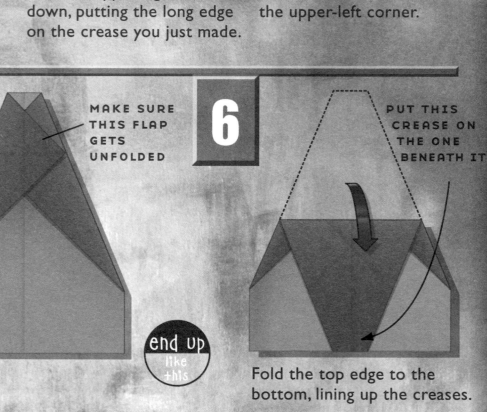

PUT THIS CREASE ON THE ONE BENEATH IT

Fold the top edge to the bottom, lining up the creases.

7

NEW UPPER-RIGHT CORNER

Fold the new upper-right corner to the center of the creased X.

Do the same on the other side.

8

UNFOLD THE LAST TWO FOLDS. IT SHOULD LOOK LIKE THIS:

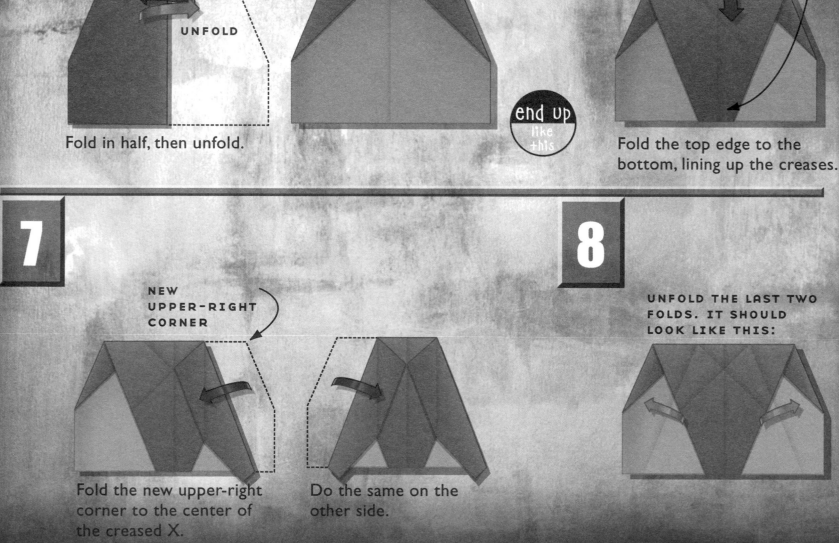

9

PUT THIS EDGE...
...ON THIS CREASE

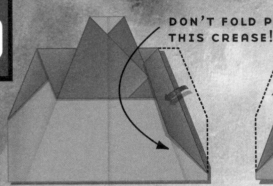

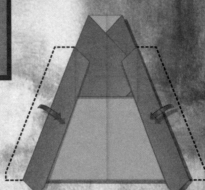

end up *like this*

Fold up on the red line as shown.

10

DON'T FOLD PAST THIS CREASE!

Fold the diagonal edge on the right side to the crease you made in step 8.

Repeat on the left side.

11

Fold both sides in along the creases you made in steps 8 and 9.

12

LINE UP THE CENTER CREASE WITH THE CREASE BELOW IT

flip over

end up *like this*

Fold the top flap down as far as it will go.

13

MAKE SURE TO LINE UP ALL EDGES

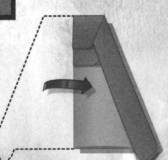

Fold in half.

14

FOLD WING EDGE TO THIS POINT

Fold the wing down so that the edge sits on the bottom corner.

flip over

Fold the other wing so it's right on top of the first.

ALMOST FINISHED

Unfold the wings so that your plane has a ∨ shape from behind.

FLYING THE HAMMER
Aim at an upward angle if you're going for distance. Throw at eye-level if you're aiming for something on the other side of the room. For everything else, chuck it as hard as you want in any direction.

game 1 / OBSTACLE GOLF

OBSTACLE GOLF

Grab a friend or two and arm yourselves with a few airplanes each. Make sure each person has a good mix of darts, gliders and stunt planes. These are your golf clubs. Then, pick a "hole" anywhere from 1 to 1,000 feet away. Good holes are things you can hit, land on, go through or pass by. Then take turns throwing a plane toward the hole, keeping track of the number of throws it takes to get there. You can switch to a different plane whenever you want, as long as you throw it from the same spot. Choosing the right plane for each throw will really help your game. And, just like in golf, low score wins.

GOOD OBSTACLE GOLF HOLES:

- *Through a basketball hoop*
- *On a shelf*
- *Caught in a tree*
- *Through monkey-bars*

- *In a clean trash can*
- *Through a window*
- *Stuck in a chain-link fence*
- *Hit a street sign*

a crash course in flight

LIFT	GRAVITY	FORCE	THRUST	DRAG
L ↑	G ↓	F ↑	T ⇨	D ➔

LIFT VERSUS GRAVITY

Without a throw, a dropped piece of paper — even one that looks like an airplane — falls right to the ground. But throw it and something holds it in the air a little longer. That something is "lift" and it's a force, just like gravity. In flight, lift and gravity play tug-of-war with your poor plane. And so long as lift is winning, the plane goes up. But when gravity takes the lead — and it always does — your plane has a date with the ground that it just won't miss.

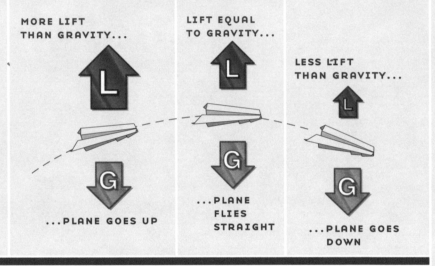

MORE LIFT THAN GRAVITY... ...PLANE GOES UP

LIFT EQUAL TO GRAVITY... ...PLANE FLIES STRAIGHT

LESS LIFT THAN GRAVITY... ...PLANE GOES DOWN

ANGLE OF ATTACK

The incline a plane's wings make with the oncoming air is called the "angle of attack." For most planes, the front of the wings is higher than the back. So, when you throw the plane, the rush of air hits the bottom of the wing and bounces off. The bouncing-off air pushes the wing upward, giving the plane lift.

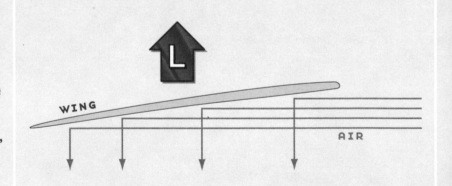

WING

AIR

ELEVATORS & AILERONS

The flaps on the back edge of a wing change the angle of oncoming air and move the plane. If the flaps go up, air hits them and goes shooting skyward. This makes the back edge of the wing drop. The angle of attack gets bigger, so more air hits the bottom of the wings. The result? The plane gets more lift and flies higher.

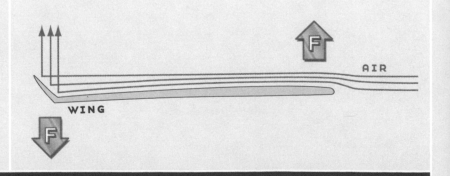

WING

AIR

SO WHY THE ⋁-SHAPED WINGS?

If your plane is flying straight, then the lift created by each wing is about the same. But if one wing is flatter than the other, that wing creates more lift and makes the plane barrel-roll. The reason most paper planes fly best with ⋁-shaped wings is that as soon as the plane starts to roll, the now-flatter wing makes more lift than the angled one. The extra lift forces the wing back up, straightening out the plane. With ⋀-shaped wings, a small roll causes a bigger roll and the plane spirals to the ground.

⋁-SHAPED WINGS SELF-CORRECT ⋀-SHAPED WINGS SELF-DESTRUCT

going.... going.... gone.

THRUST VERSUS DRAG

While gravity and lift control a plane's altitude, stuff engineers call "thrust" and "drag" change its speed.

Thrust is any force that makes an airplane go forward. In metal planes, propellers and jets create thrust. The only thrust a paper plane gets, though, comes from your own arm. Once the plane leaves your hand, it's gotten all the thrust it's going to get, which is why paper planes always end up on the ground.

Drag, on the other hand, is what air does to a plane to slow it down. The faster a plane goes, the more air hits it and the more the air pushes it backwards. And the bigger the wings are, the more air hits the plane, causing more drag. That's why glider-type paper planes go slower than darts. If a plane kept getting enough thrust to overcome both gravity and drag, it would simply keep going and going and going and going and going and going

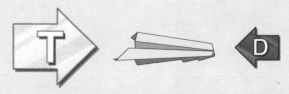

Small Wings = Less Drag = Faster

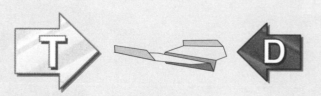

Big Wings = More Drag = Slower

The Pteroplane

TYPE: **stunt**

FOLDING DIFFICULTY: **4**

FLY ZONE:
indoor 🏠
✓ outdoor ☀️

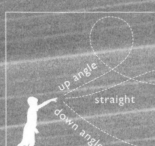
Pteroplane

The Pteroplane should have been born a dart. Instead, it's just about the quickest stunt plane anywhere. With a rocket-fuel throw, you can get it to loop, circle, even corkscrew before settling into a long, cool glide.

end up like this

CENTER CREASE

1

start like this

2

FOLD

UNFOLD

Fold and unfold lengthwise to make a center crease.

3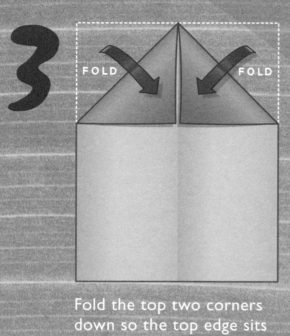

FOLD   FOLD

Fold the top two corners down so the top edge sits exactly on the center crease.

4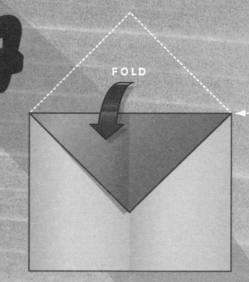

FOLD

FOLD THIS CREASE AS CLOSE AS YOU CAN TO THE FLAPS YOU JUST MADE

Fold the top point down on the center crease.

5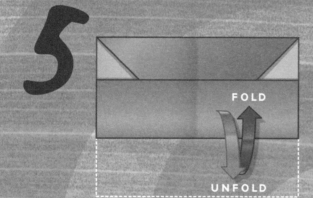

FOLD

UNFOLD

flip over

end up like this

Fold the bottom of the paper up, making a crease right at the tip of the upside-down triangle. Unfold.

6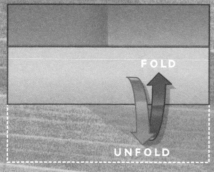

FOLD

UNFOLD

flip over

end up like this

Fold the bottom up along the same crease. Unfold again.

look out, a dino-soar!

37

7

USE SCISSORS IF YOU HAVE TROUBLE TEARING THE PAPER

Gently tear the paper along the crease.

end up like this

SMALL RIPS ARE OKAY

BIG ONES AREN'T

Tear slowly until the bottom of the paper is completely removed. Don't throw it away!

8

POINT TOUCHES TOP

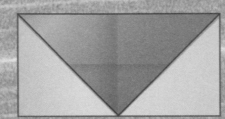

end up like this

Fold the point to the top edge, right on the center crease. Unfold.

 Pay attention. this is tricky!

9

FOLD

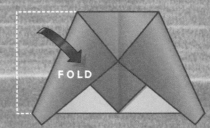

FOLD

Fold the top right corner to the + formed by the creases in the middle.

Do the same with the top-left corner.

10

THIS FLAP SHOULD BARELY COVER...

...THE FLAPS YOU JUST MADE

Fold the point in the middle up as far as it will go. Crease well and unfold.

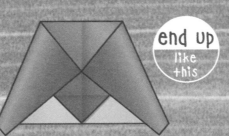

end up like this

11

THE CREASE YOU JUST MADE

FOLD

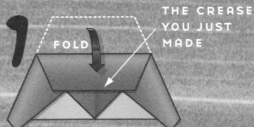

Put the top edge of your plane on the crease you just made. Line it up and crease carefully.

12

flip over

Flip the tip back up along the same crease.

end up like this

13

LINE UP ALL THE EDGES

FOLD

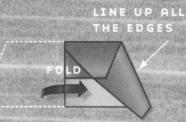

Fold in half, left to right.

14

FOLD

Grab the piece of paper you tore off in step 7. Fold it in half lengthwise.

15

Carefully tear the strip in half along the up-and-down center crease.

16
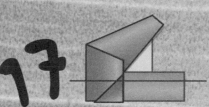

end up like this

Tuck one of the pieces into the top flap of the plane's body. (Throw the other piece away.)

17
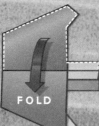
FOLD

flip over

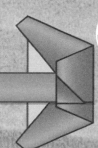

end up like this

Fold the wing so that a pinky's width of the tail gets folded over. Make the crease parallel to the body.

18
FOLD

Fold the other wing down so it matches the one below it.

ALMOST FINISHED

Unfold so your Pteroplane looks like this from the back.

FLYING THE PTEROPLANE
Your best flights will be hard throws up and away from you. Put an elevator in one wing for circles and corkscrews, and in both wings for loops.

TYPE: glider/dart/ stunt

FOLDING DIFFICULTY: **2**

FLY ZONE:
indoor 🏠
outdoor ☀

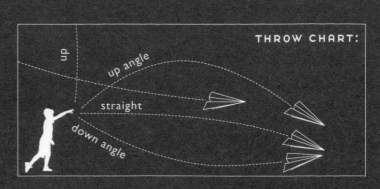

THROW CHART:

up

up angle

straight

down angle

THE PROFESSIONAL

THIS IS THE BEST ALL-AROUND PAPER AIRPLANE WE'VE EVER SEEN. IT'S EASY TO FOLD, DURABLE AND FLIES LIKE A PRO. WITH A LITTLE FUSSING, **THE PROFESSIONAL** WILL FLY LIKE A GLIDER, A DART, EVEN A STUNT PLANE. WHEN YOU NEED A PAPER PLANE THAT ABSOLUTELY, NO-QUESTIONS-ASKED ENDS THE COMPETITION — YOU NEED **THE PROFESSIONAL.**

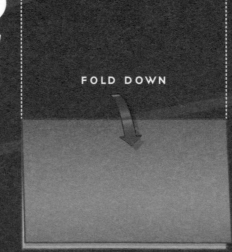

1

start like this

2

FOLD DOWN

Fold in half, top to bottom. Be exact.

3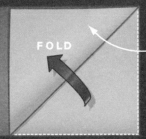

FOLD

FOLD JUST THE TOP LAYER

Fold the right edge of the top flap up so it sits on the crease you just made.

4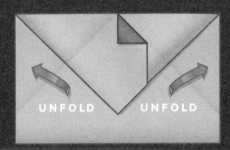

FOLD UP

Make the same fold with the left edge. The top half of the paper should look like an upside-down triangle.

5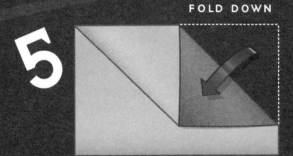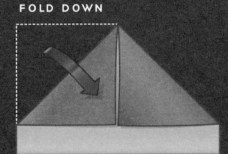

FOLD DOWN   FOLD DOWN

UNFOLD   UNFOLD

Fold the upper-right corner down to the tip of the upside-down triangle.

Do the same with the upper-left corner.

Unfold the last two folds you made.

folding tip

this is tricky, follow the drawings carefully!

6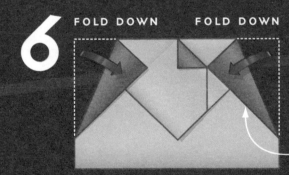

FOLD DOWN   FOLD DOWN

BRING THE EDGES ALMOST, BUT NOT QUITE, TO THE CREASES

Fold the right and left corners down to the creases you just unfolded.

7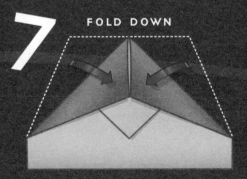

FOLD DOWN

Refold along the same creases.

8

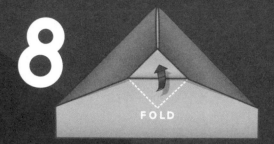

FOLD

flip over

end up
like this

Fold the point in the middle up.

9

LINE UP ALL THE EDGES BEFORE YOU CREASE YOUR FOLD

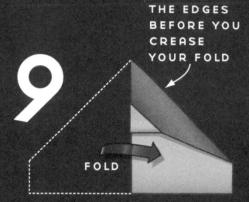

FOLD

Fold in half, from left to right.

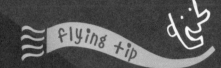

flying tip

You'll need to put elevators in the professional's back wings. See page 9 to learn how.

See page 9 to learn how.

10

FOLD THE WINGS ROUGHLY ALONG THIS LINE

FOLD

Fold the top wing down as shown.

11

end up
like this

flip over

end up
like this

42

FLYING THE PROFESSIONAL
Good, solid straight-ahead throws are the Professional's fuel of choice. But increase the elevators on the back edge and aim for the sky and you'll get big, arcing loops and corkscrews. If you want a slower glide, flatten out the fins. For dart-like flights, flatten the elevators and make sure the fins stick straight up.

ALMOST FINISHED

12

FOLD

Fold the other wing right on top of the first. Line up all the edges carefully.

Unfold the wings so your plane looks like this from the back.

Make fins by folding a pinky-width of paper up on each side.

game 2 | CHASE RACE

For this game, you'll need a good arm, a straight-flying plane and a couple ready-to-run legs. Have each racer make a plane that flies straight and far.

Then, pick a starting line and a finish line at least a soccer field's length apart. Get everyone to line up on the starting line, planes in hand. When somebody yells "go," each racer throws his plane as far as he can toward the finish line, then runs after it.

The only two rules are:

1. No running with your plane.

2. Both you and your plane have to cross the finish line to win.

So throw your plane, tear off after it, throw it again, tear after it, throw it again, tear after it... until somebody wins.

Troubleshooting (better flying through fiddling)

HOW TO TWEAK YOUR PLANE'S LITTLER BITS AND GET IT TO FLY.

Even a perfectly folded plane needs a bit of fiddling to fly its best. The good news is that careful tweaking can get almost any plane in the air, perfect or not.

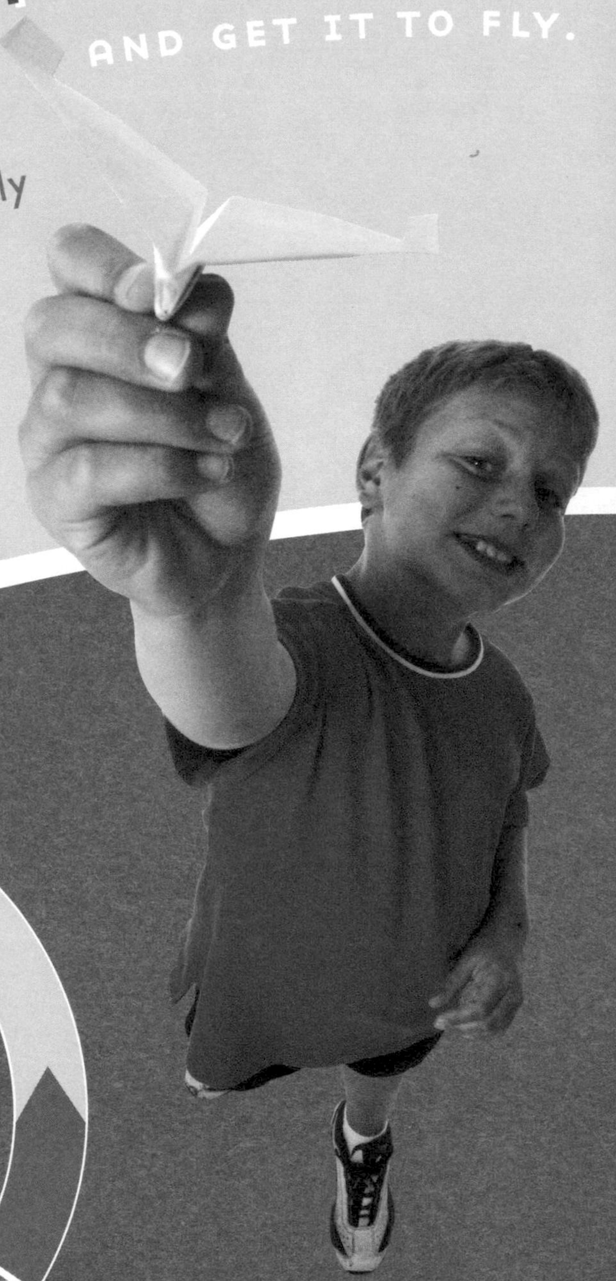

PROBLEM: I get a "rollercoaster" flight path

SOLUTION: Lower elevators or add down elevators

PROBLEM: my plane barrel-rolls to the ground

SOLUTION:

1. Make sure you have a -shaped dihedral
2. Check your plane for symmetry
3. Add or change ailerons

PROBLEM: My plane is dive-bombing

SOLUTION:

1. Ease up on your throw
2. Add up elevators

The trick to tweaking your plane correctly

is to identify, then fix, one problem at a time. For the first few throws of a newborn plane, go through a cycle of checking and fixing that looks something like this:

throw

Figure Out Problem

Fix By tweaking

More about dihedrals, elevators and ailerons on page 9

PROBLEM

My plane's flight is unstable

1. Make sure your plane has a ⌄-shaped dihedral
2. Add vertical fins to your plane's wings (see page 17, Spy Plane)

SOLUTION

PROBLEM

It always turns in the same direction

1. Make sure your plane is symmetrical and fix any differences
2. Raise the aileron on the wing opposite the direction you want your plane to turn

SOLUTION

PROBLEM

My plane rolls over and flies upside-down

Lift the wings to get a ⌄-shaped dihedral

SOLUTION

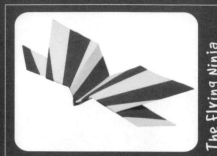

The Flying Ninja

TYPE: **stunt**

FOLDING DIFFICULTY: **4**

FLY ZONE: ✓ indoor 🎁 ✓ outdoor ☀

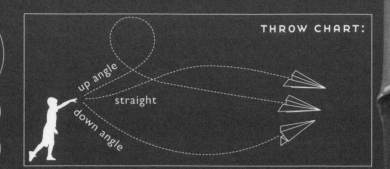

up angle
straight
down angle

THE FLYING NINJA

The Flying Ninja is a fast, sharp-looking, tight-cornering stunt plane. It's as quick and unpredictable indoors as out, and guaranteed to turn heads — or slice them off.

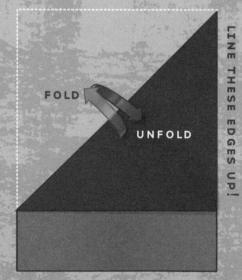

1 start like this

Pick up this corner and put it near the **X**.

X

2 LINE THESE EDGES UP!

FOLD UNFOLD

Make a diagonal crease. Then unfold it.

LINE THESE EDGES UP!

FOLD UNFOLD

Do the same thing with the other corner. Fold and unfold.

3

flip over

end up
like
this

You should now have a big creased X in your paper.

4

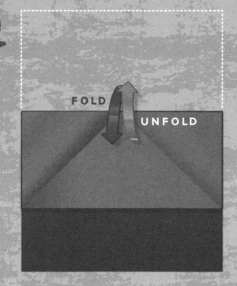

FOLD
UNFOLD

Fold the top of your paper down so that the corners line up precisely with the bottom of the creased X. Unfold.

5

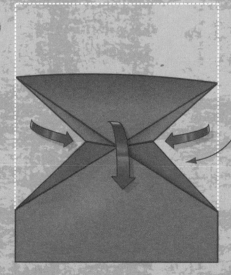

flip over

After you flip the paper over, lay it down on the table.

PRESS HERE... AND THE SIDES WILL POP UP

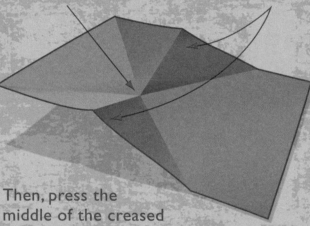

Then, press the middle of the creased X until the sides "jump" up.

6

BRING THE SIDES FORWARD AND TOGETHER

end up
like
this

Pull the top edge of the paper downward. As you do, the sides of the paper should fold inward along the horizontal crease you already made.

7

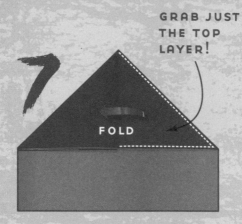

GRAB JUST THE TOP LAYER!

FOLD

Bring the bottom-right corner of the triangle over to the bottom-left corner and crease.

8

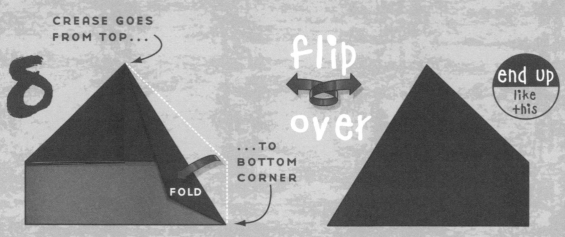

CREASE GOES FROM TOP...

...TO BOTTOM CORNER

FOLD

flip over

end up like this

Fold the the new bottom-right corner of the triangle in so that the crease runs from the top of the triangle to the lower-right corner of the paper.

9

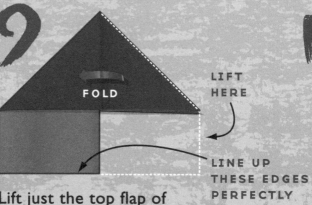

FOLD

LIFT HERE

LINE UP THESE EDGES PERFECTLY

Lift just the top flap of paper on the right side of the plane. Fold it to the left side, lining up the bottom edges of the paper.

10

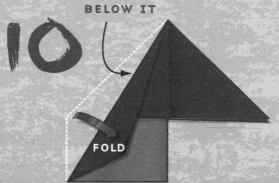

MAKE THIS CREASE RIGHT ON THE ONE BELOW IT

FOLD

end up like this

Fold the left corner of the triangle in, just like you did in step 8. Make sure it's right on top of the first one.

Without making any new folds, unfold the center creases until it looks like this.

11

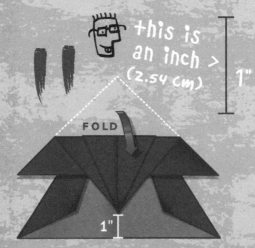

this is an inch > (2.54 cm)

1"

FOLD

1"

Fold the top of the triangle down so that it sits on the center crease, about an inch from the bottom.

12

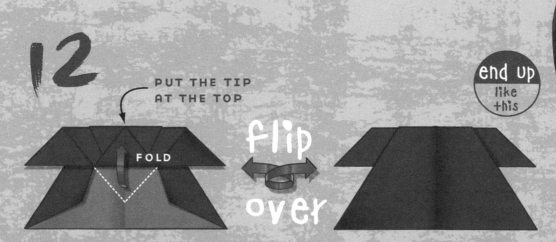

PUT THE TIP AT THE TOP

FOLD

flip over

end up like this

Flip the same flap up so that the point sits on the crease at the top.

13

FOLD

Fold the plane in half from left to right. Line up all edges perfectly.

14

NOSE

FOLD

BUTT

Fold the wing at a sharp angle, as shown. (The butt should be about twice the size of the nose.)

end up like this

The edge of the wing and the body of the plane should be roughly parallel.

15

flip over

FOLD

Fold the second wing, lining it up exactly on top of the first.

ALMOST FINISHED

Unfold the wings so it looks like this from the back.

FLYING THE FLYING NINJA

Just aim anywhere between eye level and straight-to-the-heavens, then haul off. Put some elevators on the back edge of the wings if you want small, tight loops.

49

TYPE: glider

FOLDING DIFFICULTY: **4**

FLY ZONE: indoor 🏠

outdoor ☀

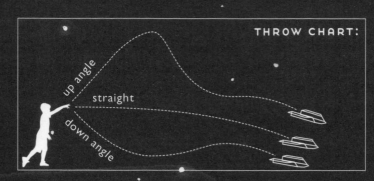

THROW CHART:

up angle

straight

down angle

THE SPACE CRUISER

THE SPACE CRUISER IS A LAZY, GRACEFUL GLIDER WITH FAR-OUT STYLING. GOOD FOR LONG, SLOW CIRCLES AROUND THE ROOM AND LOTS OF "OOH"S AND "AH"S.

1

start like this

Pick up this corner and put it near the **X**.

X

2

LINE THESE EDGES UP!

FOLD

UNFOLD

LINE THESE EDGES UP!

FOLD

UNFOLD

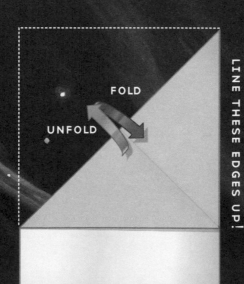

Make a diagonal crease, putting the top edge on the left. Unfold.

Do the same thing with the other corner. Fold and unfold.

3

flip
over

THIS HAS BEEN
FLIPPED OVER

You should now have a big
creased X in your paper.

4

UNFOLD

FOLD

Fold the top of your paper
down so that the corners
line up precisely with the
bottom of the creased X.
Unfold.

PRESS HERE... AND THE SIDES WILL POP UP

5

flip
over

After you
flip the paper over,
lay it down on the table.

Then, press
the middle of
the creased X
until the sides "jump" up.

6

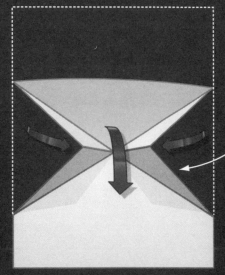

BRING THE SIDES FORWARD AND TOGETHER

end up like this

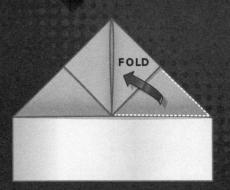

Pull the top edge of the paper downward. As you do, the sides of the paper should fold inward along the horizontal crease you already made.

7

FOLD

FOLD

Pick up just the top layer of the big triangle, folding the bottom-left corner to the top.

Do the same with the other side. Make sure to pick up just the top layer.

8

DON'T FOLD PAST THE CENTER CREASE!

FOLD

FOLD

Fold the flap up again, putting the bottom edge on the center crease.

Then fold the other flap the same way.

PUT THE POINT EXACTLY ON THE CENTER CREASE

FOLD

HOLD HERE... AND PULL OUT THIS FLAP

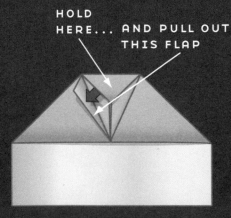

9

Fold the point down along the top of the flaps you just made.

While holding the triangle flat, hook your finger under the left flap. Pull just the top flap out from under the triangle.

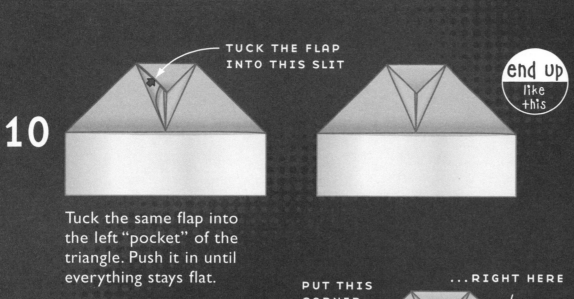

10

Tuck the same flap into the left "pocket" of the triangle. Push it in until everything stays flat.

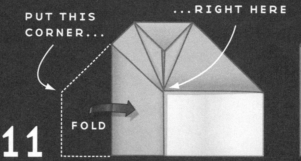

11

Fold the left edge to the center of the plane. Make sure all your edges line up.

Do the same with the right side of the plane.

12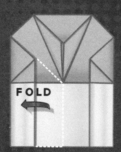

Fold the same edge back to the crease you just made.

Repeat on the left side.

ALMOST FINISHED

Straighten the wings so that your Cruiser looks like this from behind.

 FLYING THE SPACE CRUISER
To fly the Space Cruiser, chomp on the back half with your hand, just like it's getting eaten by a giant sock-puppet alien. Then, instead of throwing it, give it a good push and let go. If all goes well, it should escape your hungry alien hand and glide gently to earth.

TYPE: **toy**

FOLDING DIFFICULTY: **3**

FLY ZONE:
indoor 🏠
outdoor ☀

THROW CHART:

straight

the hurricane

This is the world's only gotta-barrel-roll-to-fly paper airplane. Not only can it turn over and over and still fly, but it won't do it any other way. It's a great plane for a game of catch, a bit of flying or when you just have to have the weirdest plane in the sky.

1

start
like
this

2

FOLD

UNFOLD

Fold in half lengthwise. Unfold to make a center crease.

CENTER CREASE

end up
like
this

3

CENTER CREASE

FOLD

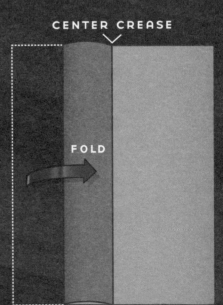

Bring the left edge to the center crease and fold.

4

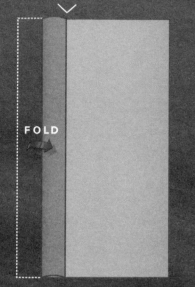

CENTER CREASE

FOLD

Fold the new left edge to the same crease and flatten well.

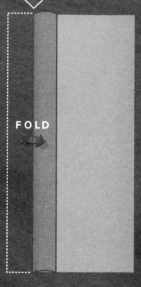

CENTER CREASE

FOLD

Then refold the center crease.

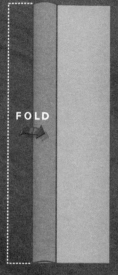

FOLD

Fold the same bundle one more time.

5

PULL THE PAPER ACROSS AN EDGE TO MAKE IT CURL

ALMOST FINISHED

A BIT OF TAPE CAN KEEP IT FROM UNWRAPPING!

Following the direction of the curl, form the paper into a tube. Tuck the corner of the right-hand end under the lip of the other end. Overlap the ends by a thumb-width.

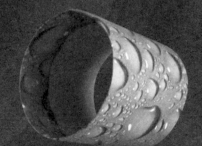

flying tip Put your index finger on the back edge of the tube and give it a push at the end of your throw.

FLYING THE HURRICANE
If you can throw a football, you can fly the Hurricane. Palm the outside, with the folded end facing away from you. Then throw it at medium speed with a little spin. The trick to getting spin is to flick your fingers toward the ground while you release the throw. If it's got enough forward movement and enough spin, it should corkscrew up and away.

credits

LEAD DESIGN
Anne Schultz

DESIGN
Andrew Wicklund
Kevin Plottner
William Keats

HOT AIR
John Cassidy

ART DIRECTION
Jill Turney

PAPER CUT PROVIDER
Kelly Shaffer

AIR TRAFFIC CONTROL
Gary Mcdonald

ILLUSTRATION
COVER ART
John Walker
Steve Kongsle *(the wind beneath our wings)*
TECH ART
Teshin Associates
Doug Stillinger
ADDITIONAL ART
Liz Hutnick
Andrew Wicklund

PHOTOGRAPHERS
Peter Fox
Joseph Quever
Tom Upton

FLIGHT ATTENDANT
Megan Smith

SPECIAL THANKS
Eiji Nakamura for the Nakamura Lock
Steve Pease
Andrew Flautt
Kelsey Stillinger

MODELS
Benito Amaral
Scott Baer
Ryan Bell
Travis Bowers
John Christopherson
Kristen Dauler
James David
Stuart Dooley
Jenner Fox
Nick Godin
Marisa Kanemoto
Young Kuk Lee
Patrick Long
Erin McGovern
Chelsea McLaughlin
Camden Santo
Michael Starr
Hrishikesh Srinagesh
Nicholas Tumminaro
Scott White
Allison Wyndham
Jonathan Zeglin